The Condemned

A memoir told through selected early works of short stories, essays, and poetry

By: Shari Lopatin

BookBooks Publishing LLC

Published by: BookBooks Publishing LLC, Phoenix, Arizona
Cover Artwork by: Simona Catena
Cover Design by: Marta Obucina
Formatted by: Emmanuel Okpeniku

(E-Book) ISBN-13: 978-0-9997827-2-9
(Paperback) ISBN-13: 978-0-9997827-3-6

First Edition
Printed in the United States

Visit the author's website at www.ShariLopatin.com

Other Works by Shari Lopatin

The Apollo Illusion

• ACKNOWLEDGEMENTS •

I had a wonderful production team behind me to produce this book, and I could not have accomplished publication without them.

I want to thank Simona Catena for her beautiful and amazing artistic talent in conceptualizing and creating my book's cover art. I also want to thank Marta Obucina for her incredible skills in designing my book's cover. And finally, I want to thank Emmanuel Okpeniku for his sharp eye and precision in formatting my book's interior pages.

I also could not have completed this project without the support of my family: my parents Jill and Jerry Lopatin, my sister Rebecca Lopatin, my love and partner Oscar Barrascouth, and my favorite writing partners (a.k.a. my cats) Teddi Bear and Ferdinand.

Finally, I want to thank all the reviewers, readers, book-lovers, and small-time booksellers who buy my work, subscribe to my newsletter, tell their friends about my writing, and help support the indie author community. You made this possible for a writer like me; thank you!

• CONTENTS •

For my parents, Jill and Jerry Lopatin

Letter from the Author

My Dear Reader,

I come to you with a special type of memoir, told through the words of my earlier self via fictional short stories, non-fiction essays, and poetry. I never intended for the bits and pieces to come together someday, but they did—unexpectedly.

As the crux of the COVID-19 pandemic began winding down, and my traumatized brain started thinking creatively again, I began going through my life's archive of (mostly) unpublished work with the hopes of reigniting my writing muscle. To my surprise, I'd written a vast amount of *stuff* in the first twenty years of my formative life that spanned historical events like the Great Recession and September 11, as well as personal injustices like Antisemitism.

I found poems from as early as high school, MySpace rants from my early twenties, and short stories from my early thirties. As I started reading them, I detected some common themes and realized when combined, these writings revealed the larger story of my earlier self—a millennial coming of age through the 1990s and 2000s while navigating typical young adult issues exasperated by The Great Recession, the aftermath of September 11, and the effects of (what I've now come to understand was) Antisemitism.

Today, in my forty-first year, I decided to select and lightly edit the best essays, poems, and fictional short stories from that earlier period in my life—lasting between ages fifteen and thirty-five, respectively—and publish them in this collection.

One of the short stories I decided to publish is called, "The Condemned," which I chose as the namesake of this book. "The Condemned" is the most autobiographical fiction story I've written to-date, and while that played a role in my decision to use its title for this book, it's not the primary reason. "The Condemned" represents the most common theme I noticed throughout my earlier works:

I often felt condemned in one way or another.

Whether it was from heartbreak, ostracization, disillusionment, the search for home, loss and death, or mental health challenges, I often found myself feeling *othered*.

However, through those feelings, I also found something hopeful: a stronger sense of self-acceptance, inner truth, and eventually, other types of love, including self-love and romantic.

May you find empathy, understanding, solidarity, strength, and even healing in these writings from my earlier self. And whether you're starting adulthood or recalling earlier days—like me—may you never stop seeking truth and find your own sense of love through these words, for love is the ultimate binder of us all.

Yours truly,
Shari

The Condemned

A memoir told through selected early works of short stories, essays, and poetry

FICTIONAL SHORT STORIES

• POMEGRANATES •

> "The language of friendship is not words, but meanings."
> **– Henry David Thoreau**

~~~

They say Arizona is a place for folks to start over, and that's what I had in mind when I landed in the high desert of Prescott. I remember, it was the year the sun rose red over the United Kingdom, and boilin' wine flowed across the hills of Northern California.

It was also the year I met Helen.

Folks like me don't like other folks' judgmental stares, so we stay indoors and keep to ourselves. I didn't have no friends to help me move into my two-bedroom duplex that Saturday afternoon, when Thanksgivin' was in the air and cool crispness stung my cheeks. I was liftin' boxes from my pickup truck into an empty livin' room when I heard her voice before I saw her face.

"Howdy there, neighbor," she said, and her voice was wispy. I put down my box onto the dirt driveway, and when
~~~

I turned around, she was starin' at me with a hand on her hip, silver hair cropped above her ears.

"Hi," I said, suspicious.

"You need some help?"

"What's it to ya?"

She smiled, and I watched her leathery skin crinkle at the corners of her eyes. "Just helpin'," she said. "My name's Helen, and this here's Baby Ruth; she's my best friend." Helen motioned down to her feet at a black cat with yellow eyes, a tiny thing, probably the runt of the litter. "She follows me everywhere, just like a dog."

"Nice to meet y'all," I said, as the cat came to rub against my legs. I didn't have much experience with animals, so I didn't pet her. But the way she looked at me, with those easy goin' eyes, it triggered some long-buried emotion that I couldn't name.

"Why Baby Ruth?" I asked.

"'Cause that's the best damn candy bar ever made by mankind. And it fits her, don't ya think?"

The cat meowed. "Sure, I suppose," I said.

"What's your name?"

I froze, never big on sharin' personal details right away. A girl can never be too careful.

"Jessie," I said after a few moments. "Jessie Jay Jones." I bit my lip for givin' her my full name, unsure why I did it.

"Well ain't that a pretty name," Helen responded, crackin' a smirk. "So back to my original question, Miss Jessie Jay Jones: do you need some help?"

I was going to tell her no, that I got it myself, that I was used to bein' on my own, but I said yes. That afternoon, Helen and her black cat, Baby Ruth, helped me move into my patio home. It was the first time in my life that anyone lent a hand liftin' my old, ratty boxes.

***

Helen lived directly across the street from me. I could see straight into her front window if I wanted, but I wasn't much for spyin'. She told me she lived there for fifteen years. Gosh dang, I was still in middle school when Helen moved into that house. I couldn't imagine livin' *anywhere* for fifteen years.

Like me, she lived alone, except for Baby Ruth. But there was always these cars comin' and goin' from her house, and people—all *kinds* of people: Mexicans and artists and ranchers. One day, a lady showed up who claimed to be Helen's best friend from childhood. She was a Wiccan, and when Helen introduced us, she taught me all about the red candles and black candles and white candles.

I wanted to ask Helen where she was from, what she did, but I feared bein' intrusive. I hated when people intruded into my life, so I never asked. Helen, on the other hand, wasn't so shy.

"What do you do?" she inquired one day.

"For a livin'?"

"Of course for a living."

"Oh, it ain't nothin' special," I told her. "I just work at the local diner."

"As a waitress?"

"Pretty much."

"You got a boyfriend?"

I shook my head. "Naw," I said.

"Why not?"

I shrugged my shoulders and looked down at Baby Ruth, who was restin' comfortably on Helen's feet. "Guess I just move around too much."

I anticipated the judgement any moment.

"A girl shouldn't spend too much time alone," Helen said, and I grimaced.

"You're alone," I said, my voice a little sharp, and then I felt bad. Somethin' told me Helen didn't say it out of shrewdness, but rather, out of concern.

"So it would seem," she responded. Then Helen smiled, but I noticed it wasn't genuine. Instead, she seemed—robotic. "But honey, I ain't *never* alone."

That night, after I came home from another shift of crappy tips and crabby parents and cat-callin' married men, I felt an episode comin' on. It always started with a pit of dread in my gut, like a killer was waitin' to pounce from the shadows of my closet.

Then I got paranoid, switchin' on every light and peeking 'round every corner I could find. The thoughts started racin', attacking my mind like a swarm of bees, and I started seein' red, looming and woeful, and it frightened me.

"You ain't no good at nothin', Jessie Jay."

"If no black eyes are gonna teach you respect, maybe they'll knock some sense into you."

"Gosh dang it, Jessie Jay. The least you can do is give me a blowjob if you can't cook a meal."

I always felt like I was gonna die. I stopped breathin' and my knees went weak, so I fell to the floor and wondered if I'd be alone for the rest of my life, even though I liked bein' alone. I hated myself for wantin' more, for wishin' my family was there, even when my family was mean.

I wanted it to stop every time, so I cried some more, pleadin' into the open air. When the pain kept on comin', I closed my eyes and started wailin' harder, convulsin' and clenchin' my muscles until finally, I fell asleep on the floor. I didn't remember nothin' after that.

The doorbell roused me the next mornin'. I'd spent all night on the floor in a fetal position and drooled on the carpet. My neck was killin' me too. When I called out to ask who's there, silence responded.

I pushed myself to a sittin' position, then climbed to my feet. I stumbled to the front door, the taste of yesterday's food still in my mouth, and glanced out the window. Empty air.

I opened the door—looked left, then right—and finally I glanced down. When I first saw it, I remember feelin' confused.

A bag of fresh pomegranates.

I reached to grab the bag, unsure at first what I was holdin', and a note fell from the inside. I snagged it before the wind could, and opened the folded paper.

Please enjoy some fresh pomegranates from my backyard tree. It always produces more fruit than I can eat. Let me know if you'd like more. I have plenty.

Happy Thanksgiving!

Helen

I almost dropped the pomegranates. No one had ever left fruit at my doorstep before, and as I stared at the bag of orbs, I broke down cryin'.

I pulled the fruit inside and closed the door, cradlin' the pomegranates like new kittens. When I peered out my front window, I saw Helen wearin' heavy gardening gloves and clearin' away brush as Baby Ruth trotted behind her. I studied her movements, her facial expressions, her keenness. She was a cross between Annie Oakley and Mary Poppins, filled with grit and mystery, but also compassion.

I started to wonder about Helen's life, her travels, her story. I didn't even know her last name.

I'll ask her soon, I told myself. *I'll ask her soon.*

***

Thanksgivin' came and went, and soon Christmas would arrive. The holiday was maybe two weeks away when Helen had her first garage sale since I moved in.

"Where'd you get all this *stuff*?" I asked, crossin' the street to examine her multitude of trinkets, crafts, and quilts.

"I made it," Helen said.

"All of it?"

"You better believe it."

Baby Ruth wandered up to say hello, and I reached down to scratch her chin.

"She's taken a liken' to you," Helen said.

"Well, she is a cute little thing. How'd you meet her?"

"Found her in my garage when she was a kitten. Her momma'd been attacked by coyotes and dragged her to my place. That poor mamma, she died a day later, so I bottle-fed Baby Ruth back to health. She's been by my side ever since. That was what—ten years ago now?"

"What a great story," I said, and knelt down to Baby Ruth's level. She hopped onto my knee and I found myself gigglin'.

"She only does that when she's really fond of someone," Helen said.

I pet Baby Ruth and reveled in her gentle purrs. When she jumped off, I stood again. "Do you mind if I look around at your work?" I asked. "Maybe I'll buy somethin'."

"Sure, take your time."

I began pokin' through Helen's garage and found myself tantalized by her crafts. Beautiful scarves knitted with expertise, wall-sized quilts stitched with scenes of sunsets and Saguaros, finely painted birdhouses, bronze-welded windchimes. It went on and on and on.

"Where did you learn to do this?" I asked, fascinated.

"My momma encouraged it," she said, but didn't reveal more. "The Mexicans, they like to come here on Fridays and buy in bulk, then sell south of the border."

"You ever been to Mexico?"

I waited for an answer, but Helen only winked at me. "How are those pomegranates?" she asked.

I wished she'd answer my question, but I didn't want to be annoyin', so I let it go.

"They're delicious," I said. I could tell Helen took pride in makin' others feel good and accepted. "I've been using them in salads. I'm goin' to bake you some banana bread soon, as a thank-you."

"No need. Just glad to bring a smile to your face."

I spent more time meanderin' through Helen's crafts before settlin' on the red-and-white birdhouse that hung from a yellow string. When I went to pay for it, Helen held up her hand.

"It's yours," she said. "A gift. You go on now and feed those baby birds."

I wanted to hug her, but somethin' in the way Helen spoke told me she wasn't the huggin' type. So I thanked her once again, and walked across the street back to my place.

***

I'd decided to climb into bed early that night and was already snugglin' under the covers when I heard the sirens. I lived on a quiet street in a quiet town, so the sirens caused enough concern that I crawled outta bed and into my slippers.

The air was freezin' that night, and we were expectin' the first snow. I switched on my bedroom light when I realized the sirens got louder and closer. Rubbin' my arms to stay warm, I sauntered toward the front window and looked outside. About four police cars had parked in front of Helen's house.

"What the hell?" I asked aloud, and a vile feeling rose from deep in my stomach. Somethin' was wrong.

I spun around and jogged back to my bedroom, reached into the closet, and grabbed a robe. I wrapped it around my waist before runnin' outside. The air was damp, and I could smell the snow comin'. But that didn't matter. My eyes fixated on the crime tape surroundin' Helen's house.

"What's goin' on out here?" I called, hopin' one of the officers would answer.

"Ma'am, we need you to step back please."

"That's my friend in there. Is she OK?"

Another officer approached when I said this, a tall man with copper skin. When he spoke, he revealed a thick, Spanish accent.

"You say you're her friend?" the officer asked.

"Yes sir."

"What's your name?"

"Jessie Jay Jones."

His eyes wilted when I said this, and he turned back to his partner. "This is her," he said.

By now, I was crazy confused and startin' to grow angry. Why wouldn't anyone tell me what happened? I was desperate to know if Helen was alright.

"Miss Jones, we have some difficult news," the officer said. "Your neighbor, Helen, took her life tonight."

My heart stopped beatin' the moment I heard those words. At first, I thought my mind played a cruel trick, but when I asked him to repeat himself, I knew I'd heard correctly.

"How – how is that possible?" I asked.

"She left a note," the officer continued. "And she named you."

"She named ... *me*?"

The officer bit his lip. I could tell this was hard for him. "Yes ma'am. She asked if you could take care of Baby Ruth for her. She said no girl should spend too much time alone."

I lost my balance then, and all I could think about was the heartbroken look I imagined in Baby Ruth's eyes, and I collapsed to the ground hysterical.

"How could she do this?" I asked, cryin' into my hands. "Why? *Why?*"

A woman rushed to my side, and she smelled of peppermint and vanilla. I didn't see her face, or know her name, but I felt her embrace tryin' to comfort me. I couldn't understand what had happened, why Helen would feel so badly that she'd leave Baby Ruth alone. She loved Baby Ruth with everythin' she had.

They later told me she'd downed a bottle of sleepin' pills and probably didn't feel a thing. She left behind two grown children and some grandkids who lived on a ranch in Texas. I couldn't believe my ears when I heard this. I'm from Texas, too.

I took Baby Ruth home with me that night, and she howled into the darkness. I'd never heard a cat howl in despair, and it's the most tragic sound I never want to hear again. I tried to encourage her to eat the food Helen left behind, but Baby Ruth wouldn't touch it.

I started to panic that she'd die too, but after another day, she finally nibbled. Within a week, she jumped into bed with me and we mourned together.

I stared out my front window as Helen's family arrived to clear out her house. They piled mounds of crafts into plastic crates, which they transferred into SUVs. I felt compelled to reach out and meet them, but then I grew scared and stayed inside. They probably wouldn't think much of me anyhow.

I didn't do nothin' for Christmas, besides spendin' it quietly with Baby Ruth on my lap. I thought long and hard about Helen's last message: *no girl should spend too much time alone.*

Helen always had people comin' and goin' at her house, but maybe it wasn't enough. I found myself wakin' each mornin' and starin' at her empty place, until one day, I saw myself lyin' dead in there, and it terrified me.

After the *For Sale* sign went up, I decided to check on Helen's pomegranate tree one day. I let myself into her backyard and realized how vacant it felt. The tree still had ripe fruit hangin' from its branches, so I pulled them off to keep them from rottin'.

"I never did bake you that banana bread," I said to the pomegranates as I twirled them in my palms. "I'm so sorry, Helen."

When I pulled the last of the fruit from her tree, I heard a female voice call from the front of the house askin' who was behind the gate. I didn't answer, but crept toward the front, unsure who waited on the other side. When I turned the corner, I recognized the woman from the days after Helen died, when she'd wept from the driveway. She was Helen's daughter.

"Who are you?" she asked, and I was about to run away and retreat into my duplex, but then I remembered Helen's warning. Swallowin' my nerves, I forced myself to stop and look the woman in the eyes.

"I was a friend of your momma's," I said, and the woman's expression softened immediately.

"No kiddin'?" she said. "How'd you know her?"

"I live across the street." I motioned to the patio home with Baby Ruth starin' out the window.

"Is that my momma's cat?" the woman asked.

"Yes ma'am," I said. "She asked me to care for her. I hope you don't mind."

The woman nodded, but I could tell she was conflicted, so I did somethin' I'd never done before. "You wanna come inside for some tea?" I asked. "Maybe you can tell me more about your momma."

At my offer, the woman grinned, and I realized it was the same welcomin' smile that Helen always had. "I'd love that," she said. "My name's Jeanine."

I stepped forward and shook her hand. "I'm Jessie Jay Jones."

"Now ain't that the most darlin' name I heard in a decade."

Her compliment made me feel warm inside. "Thank you," I said. "Would you like a pomegranate?"

As I handed Jeanine the fruit, I felt fear leave my mind for the first time in my life. Helen's daughter took the pomegranate from my hand, and we walked across the street together as the snow started driftin' from above.

###

Note from the author: *I dedicate "Pomegranates" to my neighbor, may she rest in peace.*

• A CALL FROM PARIS •

> *"We do not remember days, we remember moments."*
> **– Cesare Pavese**

~~~

"Do you remember when we used to talk about renting a one-bedroom apartment and saving all our money to travel the world?" she asked him.

"Yes, I do," he answered, his voice quiet on the phone.

"Do you remember when backpacking across Latin America sounded fun?"

His voice grew even quieter, now. "I do."

"Why can't we think like that, anymore?"

He sat there, pondering, the cold phone pushed against his ear. He didn't know. He didn't know what happened, or how.

"Do you remember—"

"Yes."

They were thirty-five and thirty-nine. Married for five years, together for ten. And this Tuesday night, summer
~~~

rain tapping against their four bedrooms' towering windows, they spoke countries apart. A business trip ... yet again.

She often wondered why she took them—Money, that's right. —

And he sat alone, in the dark. Just another routine weeknight. Just another routine.

"Why didn't we do it?" she continued, her voice broken by static from the long-distance phone call.

"Do what?"

"Save and travel."

"Your mother," he reminded her. "My school loans."

She sighed. And maybe wept. He couldn't be sure, because of that damn static. People who traveled lived in a bubble, he reminded himself. They lived on trust funds or skirted responsibility.

"Do you ever wish we could give it all up?" Her voice sounded serious, and for a moment, his heart jumped. He felt a tingle again, a spark of excitement.

"Give what up?"

"Everything."

He began to say yes, but something stopped him. And he sunk lower into his chair, the beginnings of a grin fading from his face. "What about the house?"

"We can rent it."

"What about our jobs? We may not find work after we come back."

"Fuck my job."

He could hear her pacing on the other side now. He knew his wife well enough to detect when the anxiety started.

"Do you remember what it felt like?" Her voice pleaded with him, begged, like a hungry man desperate for a bite of bread.

"We have responsibilities now," he reminded her, and wondered why he didn't feel heated. They'd argued like this before, and the rage always began crawling up his neck to pound at the doors of his head. But this time, it didn't. Instead he just felt ... *numb.*

"We don't have kids."

"We have cats."

"They can stay with my sister for six months."

"She's allergic."

He listened as she took a deep breath, her voice shuddering as she exhaled. "I guess you're right."

The world stopped with her words, with her surrender to his rationale. Someone was gripping his windpipe and squeezing. Cutting off the life. Why did she always have to give up on him, on them?

"How's Paris?" he asked, desperate to change the subject.

"The same as every other place."

"How can Paris possibly be the same?"

"Same room service, same limos. Same conference centers."

"You should go and visit Versailles, while you're there."

"With what free time?" Her voice snapped this time, revealing a new edge—something he'd not heard before.

"I just thought—"

"You just thought what? That even if I had free time, I'd want to go alone?"

The pit in his stomach returned. He stood from his chair and wandered to the kitchen, lights dimmed around him, rain now pounding harder outside. In the distance, thunder rolled across the valleys and quick, flashing lights illuminated the stove. He swung open the nearest cabinet and grabbed the bottle of Scotch.

"I thought you liked traveling for work," he said.

"It's not the same." Her voice was hard, and she absently played with delicate stockings and high heels. She could still recall the feeling of hiking boots and boulders under her feet.

He poured a glass full of Scotch.

"What are you doing?"

He took a large gulp, wincing as the liquor burned down his throat. "Nothing," he said. "Just drinking some water."

"Do you remember when we used to wake up at two in the morning?"

He stopped drinking for a moment.

"And photograph the meteor showers?"

"Yes."

"When was the last time we did that?"

December 14, 2010. Almost two years ago. He would never forget that night, when they made love in the back seat of their car—dynamite exploding inside of her ... jeans pushed around his ankles ... laced panties wedged into the dashboard's corner. She left for New York the next day.

"I can't remember," he said.

"Oh."

He cringed at the hurt in her voice and took another swig of Scotch, forcing it down. "When are you flying back?"

"Thursday night. Just two more days."

"And then where are you going?"

She sighed. "I don't know."

He opened his mouth to say something else, but she began speaking first. "I love you, Jason."

He hadn't heard those words in a month. The Scotch burned in his stomach and smacked him upside the head. "I – I love you too."

"You're drinking your Scotch again."

"What makes you say that?"

"Aren't you?"

He slammed the glass down and heard her breathe into the phone. The static returned, reminding him just how far away she remained.

"I was thinking," she started, "maybe after I come back, I'll quit."

"You don't want to quit." He cursed himself for speaking before thinking.

"Stop acting like you know what I want."

"What will you do?"

"Let's rent out the house. We'll move into a small apartment and save."

"We can't."

"Why not?"

"You know why."

"Fuck the why!"

She broke down into tears now. "I'm tired of the 'why.' Everything is 'why this' and 'why that.'"

"We're not trust fund babies, Renee."

The tears flowed freely now, spilling like water down a flooded river. She convulsed on the other line, squeezing delicate stockings until they ripped, staring at the flat screen television propped neatly above exquisite wood-carved drawers. White walls ... beige ceilings ... a single framed painting of a flower field.

She'd seen that same painting downstairs in the lobby. A copy.

"What do you want me to do?" he asked her, growing more desperate by the minute. He didn't want her to cry. He *hated* when she cried.

"I want 'us' back."

He shoved the Scotch aside. Was she serious?

"Take the leap with me," she begged.

"Renee—"

He looked around the house. Four bedrooms, three bathrooms. His own office and gym. Those damn school loans. Everything looked so empty in the darkness.

"Do you remember when we used to talk about renting a one-bedroom apartment, and saving all our money to travel the world?" she asked again, her voice quiet and tiny, almost scared.

He nodded in silence, and she continued. "Do you remember when backpacking across Latin America sounded fun?"

It still sounded fun, he told himself. But people who traveled lived in a bubble.

"I lied," he said.

"About what?"

"I do remember our last meteor shower together."

Even though his words slurred together from the booze, he heard her smile, if such a thing was possible. And then, she opened the door to something bigger.

"Let's do it, Jason."

It was getting late, and he had work early the next morning. The wind picked up outside, ferocious, vibrating their home's windows. And the thunder's gentle rolling now turned to crackling violence above their house.

He had to get to sleep. His school loan payment was due. So was the mortgage. But all he could think about was loading a backpack and running away to Thailand or Eastern Europe. With her.

"I don't know."

"Just say yes."

"I need to get to sleep."

She sighed, and he felt the hopelessness return to her voice. God, he needed a drink.

"OK," she said. "I love you."

"I love you, too." He heard the phone pull away from her ear. And with it, his life sunk away. A stabbing despair sliced through him then, and he suddenly called out.

"Renee!"

But she didn't hear, and the phone spit back only silence. Forcing down another gulp of Scotch, he said aloud, "I was going to tell you 'maybe.'"

###

• STONE FROM HELL •

An *Apollo Illusion* Short Story

> *"The most dangerous creation of any society is the man who has nothing to lose."*
>
> **– James Baldwin**

~~~

I watch the brown-haired man fall into the ditch below, his hands bound behind his back, and I lower the smoking gun.

I just blew a crater into his skull, and now I feel relieved. Killing didn't always have this effect on me. I vomited the first time. But now, after years of fighting to protect everything I worked to build, I've come to realize this one, single truth:

It's them ... or it's me.

This man was trying to escape. He knew the rules when he joined. Once a member, always a member. Anyone who leaves threatens our security. I can't allow that to happen.
~~~

People call me a monster, but that's because they don't have what it takes to survive. The minions today think it's OK to just fall in line, to become little bitches for the Upper Class and its sickening agenda to force anyone who's not like them into *slavery*. They don't call it slavery—I know—they say we *choose* to live like this; we're *lazy* for not trying harder.

Fuck them.

No one decides *my* fate. That's why I made the Upper Class *my* bitches, *my* slaves. That's why I created HELL.

***

I was fifteen when Jaron was born in the middle of summer during the year 2131. It was monsoon season in Phoenix, a desert inferno in Sector 1 that suffocated from weekly sandstorms that consumed the city. I wanted out, but Mom's sixteen-hour workdays never earned us enough to leave. We could barely eat.

The moon was new that Tuesday night, as if it understood the darkness which would soon sweep away my life. I was fast asleep, my government-issued contacts resting next to my bed, when a piercing shriek slammed into my head, shooting adrenaline through my blood like heroin.

A second shriek told me it was Mom.

"What's wrong?" I said, running into the shared space of our one-bedroom apartment. When I found her laying on our only couch, holding the balloon which swelled from her belly, the carpet below soaking wet, I knew.

"We gotta get to the hospital," I said. "Let me grab my contacts."

But Mom stopped me with the force of her voice. "No! I can't afford the hospital."

"You'll die if we don't go."

She shrieked again, and a wave of panic crippled my muscles. I fell to her side.

"Listen to me, Stone," she said, grabbing my wrist. Her palms were slick with sweat. "If we go to the hospital, we'll lose this apartment. They'll take it away to pay for the visit."

Her grip tightened around my malnourished bones like a tourniquet. I grimaced, but stayed by her side.

"What should I do?" I asked.

"Get your contacts. Find instructions on delivering a baby."

I protested, but she reached for my shirt to pull me closer, and I could smell the damp scent of sweat rolling off her temples. "If you don't do it, I'll die, and so will your brother."

I wanted to snap at her, *half-brother. He's my half-brother.* But now, it was my job to keep her alive.

I ran back to my room and grabbed my contacts, popping them into my eyes fast. Immediately, a three-dimensional screen appeared in the right hand corner of my vision, hanging in the air like a kite, displaying the words, *What would you like to do?*

"How do you deliver a baby?" I said, and the screen dissipated. In its place, lines and lines of links appeared before my face, and I scanned through the headlines by tapping my temple, each time highlighting a different option.

I found a set of directions from the United Council Medical Division and tapped my temple twice. For a moment, my sight turned black, and then a new world appeared around me. I was no longer in my bedroom, or even my apartment, but standing in a hospital room with a middle-aged doctor dressed in blue scrubs.

"Hello," he said. "My name is Dr. Hash. Today, I'm going to walk you through the steps of delivering a baby. If you have a loved one in labor now, you may follow along as you deliver in your home."

The instructions paused, giving me an option to combine reality with the video. I selected it, then raced around the corner back to Mom.

"I don't have gloves," I told her.

"Just do it," she said, so I did ... the blood, the screaming, the crowning, the coaxing, the umbilical cord, the cleaning.

I held Jaron in my arms before Mom ever could; she'd fallen unconscious afterwards. I wrapped him in towels and he screamed in my face. I had to admit, the kid was cute, even though I sensed he was about to ruin my life.

***

You need to get a job, Stone, Mom told me. *Jaron needs diapers.*

That was merely months after Jaron burst into existence. At the time, I was planning to start work anyway, but the money I made was going to be for me. To save for college. Because if I couldn't pay for an education, I was doomed to a life of poverty. College didn't promise anything glamourous those days, but at least with a degree, I could've afforded a roof over my head. Anything less ensured one a life of homelessness and misery.

Unable to defy Mom, I dutifully dropped out of high school and started my job as a tour guide for the Museum of Musical Instruments—the only place on Earth where real instruments still existed. I took a night shift, from nine o'clock until four in the morning—all from Mom's desk in the apartment. Every paycheck I made went to Jaron.

By the time I reached twenty-one years old, after Jaron turned six, I still found myself stuck behind a screen, narrating useless facts into visitors' ears as they strolled along the endless, glass-ridden hallways via the screen of a mobile droid.

"Tone," Jaron said from behind me, because he couldn't pronounce the "s" in my name, "why's Mom sleeping?"

I was preparing to begin my nightly shift. "'Cause she's tired. She worked all day," I said.

"I wanna tell her something."

I rolled my eyes. "Where are your contacts?"

"They hurt."

"Well, wear them. The government requires it and you can't keep talking. You'll get arrested if you talk in public. Use the messaging feature."

Jaron stepped back and wiped his hand over a head of black, greasy hair that resembled the coat of a skunk. Not that I'd ever seen a skunk, except through holograms, but I knew enough.

"I want ice-cream."

"It's almost nine o'clock."

"I want ice-cream!" Jaron's voice started escalating, so I said yeah, OK, can we wait until four in the morning? That shut him down.

Jaron left me alone for the next seven hours as I worked from Mom's desk, the crescent moon my only companion. I often watched the moon as I repeated the same script over and over again, thinking about the men who escaped this awful planet to walk on the lunar surface almost one hundred and seventy years ago. Since then, we'd never returned. Society left no room for dreams or ideals anymore.

After my shift finished at four o'clock, I walked into our only bedroom and gently shook Jaron's tiny body. He was snuggled next to Mom. He groaned, then opened an eye.

"Ice-cream?" I said.

He smiled, then hopped out of bed. Within ten minutes, he was dressed and we left the apartment—a rare occasion—and walked down the street to the ice-cream parlor. I hated going outside. The advertisements swarmed from towering billboards, assaulting anyone who passed: seductive women charming me into the latest pornographic program *(it feels as good as the real thing)*, young, handsome men coaxing me to try their energy drinks *(the ladies can't resist a six-pack)*.

All products from the Upper Class—the world's only employers, since they took over after the Virtual Revolution of 2075. For those born into money and power, the universe was their fantasy. Everyone else, like me, was left begging for a bone.

As was usual, no one was manning the ice-cream parlor when we walked inside. The city was silent all day every day, as every resident existed in a cyber-realm instead. That's what the world wanted, I often told myself. This was the result.

When we entered the ice-cream store, scanners and screens monitored the building, and a large printer rested in the room's corner. I kneeled, then looked into the device's scanner, and it read the contacts in my eyes, recording my information and pulling three units from my bank account. The contraption then printed Jaron his ice-cream, and we sat in silence as he licked the cone clean. I sometimes wondered what real ice-cream tasted like, the old kind, made from cream from cows.

It was just after five o'clock in the morning when we left and walked back to our apartment. We entered the elevator, which creaked from lack of use, and brushed through the air until we reached the tenth floor. We climbed off, walked to our unit, and that's when I noticed the door was ajar.

I furrowed my eyebrows, unclear what this meant, and waved Jaron to stay back. Cautiously, I took one step forward, then another, approaching the door like a nervous cat from the street. I reached out, tapping it open.

"Mom?" I called.

No answer.

A bowling ball dropped in my stomach. Something was wrong. I pushed past the threshold, calling her name again. Still no answer. I yelled for Jaron to stay outside, then ran past our couch and turned the corner into the bedroom.

That's where I found her. On the bed. Bound and gagged and naked ... and soaked in blood.

"Mom!" I cried, and fury exploded from my core. I lunged toward her, ripping her hands from the ropes and searching her body for any sign of life. Her skin was cold.

"Jaron," I called, choking. "Stay outside and call the police!"

I wrapped her in blankets softly and gently, so she wouldn't hurt. I leaned over her torso and placed my head on her belly, which still felt soft. "I'm so sorry, Mom," I said.

I knew I should have said those words to her while she was still breathing, when she could have felt their relief, but I was just angry, I told myself. *I never meant to be mean, Mom. I always loved you.*

Who the hell did this to her, I wanted to know? And why?

***

Within six months, they took away the apartment. Without Mom's help, my nightly shift at the museum wasn't enough to cover rent, and my worst fear came true. Jaron and I wound up squatting under an old overpass for shelter.

They never found the man who killed our mother. The cops threw the pieces together like a haphazard puzzle: some asshole predator was scanning apartments to find a vulnerable person who was alone—the contacts allow that—and when *his* contacts showed our mother's vital signs sleeping, he attacked.

I never told Jaron that Mom died because she was alone. It seemed a burden too great for any six-year-old to bear. If he'd never asked for ice-cream ...

Life under the overpass was cold, harsh. I felt like an orphan gazing through the window of a home not his. I barely slept, keeping myself alert to protect the two of us. But it was here that I also met Tio.

You hungry? The message popped into my line of vision one winter morning, as Jaron and I hunched over a burning trash can to stay warm. We'd both lost weight—me, ten pounds—since the apartment. I looked over my shoulder to find a guy, about my age, staring at me. His brown eyes squinted into the rising sun, and something about his demeanor hinted that he was the type who *survived.*

Because talking in public was illegal—still is—I nodded my head in response. Then, he messaged me again.

My name is Tio. What do you know about computers?

I responded with my message. *Everything. Why?*

You don't have to starve. There are other ways. Meet me at dusk in the alleyway three blocks from here.

Then he left. I turned to Jaron and messaged him what happened, telling him to come with me. That evening, I followed Tio's instructions and found him waiting in the exact place he'd described. He motioned for us to follow him into an apartment, and the place stank of rotten oil and unwashed feet. Here, out of the public's eye, we were free to talk without fear of arrest.

"Have you ever considered hacking?" Tio asked me.

"How would that make money?" I said.

Tio smirked, then chuckled. "I love meeting the virgins. You don't *earn* the money, sweetheart, you *steal it.* From bank accounts."

I paused and considered his proposal for a moment. "You mean, from them? From the Upper Class?"

Tio licked his lips, as if the thought aroused him in some sick, sexual way. Then he nodded. "Yup, or anyone else who happens to be nearby."

"But that's illegal. I can't risk going to jail and leaving my little brother to fend for himself."

At my response, Tio sauntered toward me, placed his hand on my shoulder, and lowered his gaze to meet mine. "Then don't get *caught,* sweetheart."

A fire unleashed inside me when he said that, raging flames no longer contained. I realized Tio was right; I was *through* being the victim of life. I glanced down at Jaron, at the slime smudged across his face, and decided it was time to fight back.

***

Over the next year, Tio taught me everything he knew about hacking into accounts and escaping before the authorities found him. Jaron sometimes sat nearby, listening with fervor.

"The faster you get in and out, the less evidence you leave behind—virtual footprints, I call them," Tio said.

I'd known some easy tricks, but this was a whole new level. Every day, I got faster, better, *richer*. Jaron and I gained weight and moved into an apartment. Tio took a cut of everything I stole and I sensed opportunity for true enterprise, but I couldn't pinpoint the idea. Not yet.

As Tio taught and fed my growing power, I began picking apart his story. It didn't come together with ease; he'd mention a name and his lips would grow stiff. I'd inquire, and he'd reveal he once had a younger brother. *Once.*

Then during a training session one day, I coaxed a full confession after he dropped one of his elusive clues.

"My high school teachers said I was a computer prodigy," he said, his callous façade starting to fade. "The banks recruited me, wanted me to protect their accounts from hackers. But I was still a kid, and they refused to pay—typical of the Upper Class—so my mom said no. That infuriated them, and they took revenge."

"How?" I asked, genuinely curious.

"On my younger brother." Tio paused, and I saw his Adam's apple protrude from his throat as he swallowed. "After that, she kicked me out, blamed me for his death. And this—everything I'm teaching you—is how I managed to survive."

Together, Tio and I built a small sanctuary at the end of the alleyway where we first met, against the brick wall which led to a basement. I didn't realize at the time, but this would later become the headquarters for HELL.

"We've made enough to buy a quantum computer," Tio told me one day. "We could double our profits."

"Can we purchase it offline?" I asked. "We shouldn't leave a footprint."

Tio nodded. "I know a guy." Then he paused. "Look at you, *sweetheart*. You've graduated from virgin, to whore."

Whore. The word reverberated through my head, penetrating like a broken record. I *was* a whore, still at the mercy of the Upper Class, of their despicable money and power and influence. What I needed to become was something indispensable. Something *crucial*.

Right now, I was the parasite. I needed to transform into the host.

***

It was two weeks before Jaron's eighth birthday that I caught Tio teaching my little brother about ports and servers and networking to hack into bank accounts. They were holed up in Tio's apartment, a pitiful box on the second floor next to our alleyway sanctuary. I wasn't in the room, but my contacts revealed what they were saying. Data filled my vision, like peering through the lens of a computer, spitting out words, heart rates, breaths per minute.

Conclusion: Jaron feeling excited, my contacts told me.

I always knew Jaron would eventually need to learn our tricks, our secrets. I just wasn't ready, so I marched up two flights of stairs and banged against Tio's door. Jaron opened it.

"What are you doing?" I asked him.

"You've been busy," Jaron said. "Tio has been teaching me how to survive."

I pushed past Jaron and found Tio sprawled across his couch, moving his hands through the air as he untangled parts and pieces of some account. I knew better than to interrupt him during a hacking job, so I stood there as he finished, gunpowder popping in my core.

"He's too young," I said, when Tio stopped. He glanced my way then stood from the couch, walked over to Jaron and rustled the hair atop my brother's head. Jaron peered at Tio with the eyes of a dog pleasing its owner.

"He's a fast learner," Tio said.

"I don't give a damn."

"Stone, it's OK." Jaron cut into the conversation and inserted himself between Tio and me. "You've been busy. Tio took me under his wing. He's like my uncle. In fact, did you know his name means 'uncle' in Spanish?"

Tio smirked at me. "Listen to your brother, *sweetheart.*"

"I won't allow you to use him for profit," I said, and noticed my voice shook. "Make me a whore, fine, but not Jaron."

"So *angry,*" Tio said, shaking his head in phony disappointment. "If you don't want to be a whore, do something about it."

I stopped. In the midst of my ire, Tio's words struck me like a hailstone to the head. *Do something about it.* I didn't want Jaron to be a whore; I didn't want my mother to be a victim. This was the answer I'd been seeking. With anyone—the government, an ex-lover, a criminal—able to access anything, what detail was missing, the part people needed?

Protection.

Protection of their privacy. Clients would pay more than *God* to keep their money, their homes, their loved ones safe. And if we provided the key to that protection with our underground hacking, no one would turn us in—ever.

"I know what we need to do," I said, my irritation turning to determination. "There's one rule. If we want to prevent getting caught, anyone who works for us can never leave."

***

Within months, our new organization was fully operational. I wanted to name it something dark, foreboding; Tio wanted the letters to have meaning.

"Hackers to End Lawless Labor," he said. "HELL."

The paradox was perfect, I told him, even if the acronym was shit. We'd create hell, to escape hell. And we'd target the Upper Class.

"How do we make them pay?" Jaron asked.

I explained the brilliance behind the scheme: first we'd attack a chosen prospect, clearing half of his accounts and sending a contractor to burglarize his home. We'd never hurt him physically, but create enough threats to scare him into action. We would then allow a week to pass before contacting the prospect through the most inconspicuous manner. After a sizable deposit, we'd provide our service. In order to remain protected, he'd pay a monthly fee. If he stopped, we'd stop, and allow the vultures to devour him while we watched.

HELL was an instant success. I found myself intoxicated by the incredible power we suddenly held over the Upper Class. Oh the joy it brought me to witness their tears as they came crawling on their knees, begging us like rats to drop a piece of cheese. For once, they could understand the havoc they wreaked upon *us*. For once, someone forced *them* to shit where they slept. I'd fantasized about such moments for years, and now, I was living my dream.

So of course, Tio—fucking *Tio*—had to go and fuck it up.

By this point, our operations had expanded to include four quantum computers and ten new employees. Word spread quickly about HELL, and some hackers traveled from overseas to join our enterprise. Everyone knew my name, and for the first time since Mom's apartment, Jaron looked at me with admiration. That, above all else, made me proud.

"I want to help someone, for free," Tio said to me one day, while we met in his quarters.

"What are you talking about?" I asked.

"There is a woman," he said, lowering his eyes. "She was raped. She came to me and asked for protection."

"Is she a member?"

Tio shook his head. "No, she's not part of the Upper Class. She's like us. That's why I want to help her."

"Absolutely not."

Tio shifted his stance. "Stone, she was *raped.* She's scared that next time, she'll be *killed.*"

"If we help one person for free, everyone will want the same. It makes us weak, vulnerable. We cannot survive if we allow ourselves to show signs of weakness. Her situation is not our problem."

Tio narrowed his eyes at me, and his glare resembled a wolf. "I heard your mother was raped and murdered in her home."

"None of your damn business."

"It *is* my business. I want to help this woman. She doesn't deserve to suffer."

"Neither do half the people out there!" I said. "Do you think my mother deserved to suffer, or me, or Jaron? Of course not, but it's a man-eat-man world, Tio, and I don't intend on getting tossed to the bottom again to scrounge for food. The answer is no."

I watched as Tio's eyes widened, his pupils dilated, and he leaned against the nearest wall. "Then I want out," he said.

"You know the rules."

"I want out, *sweetheart.*"

I didn't know what to do. Tio knew *everything* about HELL: our real names, where we lived, how we hacked. I didn't trust him. I could tell the asshole changed his heart, that he no longer agreed with how I ran things. He could go to the authorities, or take away Jaron, or, or ...

"You really want out?" I asked him, and Tio nodded his head. "Meet me in HELL's basement. You tell the team yourself."

Tio nodded again, and right as he turned to head for the door, I swung around to snatch the gun I kept hidden in my dresser drawer.

"One more thing, Tio," I said, aiming the gun at the back of his head. When Tio stopped and began to turn around, I squeezed the trigger. Blood spattered on the wall behind like paint, and Tio collapsed to the ground. I stared at him, my breath caught in my throat. His body reminded me of my mother's when I found her: unnaturally still.

The smell of burnt gunpowder made my eyes water, and then I saw something else, a small face staring at Tio. A younger face. A tortured face.

"How could you!" It was Jaron, and his eight-year-old voice cracked. He was peeking through the threshold, obviously coming to visit Tio.

"Jaron," I said, stepping toward him. "I ... he wanted to leave HELL."

I noticed a small speck of blood between Jaron's eyes, and he wiped it away with such force, I worried he'd tear off his skin.

"I hate you! You're *not* my brother."

Before I could say another word, Jaron vanished from Tio's apartment, and sickness slammed into me. I tasted the bile rising in the back of my throat and collapsed onto my knees, vomiting it up. I kept my eyes closed so I didn't have to face what I'd just done.

Congratulations Stone, I thought. *You're now officially a murderer.*

***

Today, it's the year 2150. The brown-haired man, who I just executed, joins dozens of other lifeless bodies in the pit below. I don't know how many men I've killed over the years; I lost count long ago. But each corpse in HELL's hole—as I call it—ensures one less threat to me and my empire.

Soon after I killed Tio, Jaron disappeared. I spent years searching for him, but never knew where he went. The first time he randomly appeared at my doorstep, I grabbed him and held on, but then he disappeared again the next day.

He returned a few years later for another short time, and I learned he's living somewhere else now, some mysterious city or society which he refuses to share. He never stays long, but at least he re-emerges for a visit sporadically. I try to track him each time he leaves, but the brainiac learned how to disconnect from the system. He outsmarted me. He outsmarted HELL.

People call me a monster, but that's because they don't have what it takes to survive. This is the world they chose. Now deal with it.

###

Note from the author: *"Stone from HELL" is a genesis story of one of the supporting characters and villains from my debut novel,* The Apollo Illusion.

• THE CONDEMNED •

"Never forget what you are, for surely the world will not. Make it your strength. Then it can never be your weakness. Armour yourself in it, and it will never be used to hurt you."

– George R.R. Martin

~~~

Ever since I was a young kid, I've been going straight to hell.

That's what tends to happen when you grow up as the only Jewish girl in the Southwest, wandering among a sea of blond heads and blue eyes. My mom used to say, "It looks like everyone is part of a cult out here."

I never really noticed, but perhaps my parents picked up on the oddness because where they grew up—Queens, New York—the streets were like a rainbow. But here in Phoenix, Arizona, everyone was golden.

So naturally, once I got to high school, I started dying my hair blond and trying to straighten its spirals with an iron. I even begged my mom to buy me some blue contacts
~~~

because I was sick of my hazel eyes. Boys only wanted to date blond cheerleaders.

But I was a dark writer.

The dates never came and my inevitable destination to hell remained consistently prevalent. You must be wondering why I'm so stuck on this notion of burning for eternity. Here's the deal: it started in the second grade, with a kid named Carl. Of course, he was blond.

"My mom says you're Jewish," he said, dangling those dopey legs from his desk chair after the teacher rearranged our seating assignments.

"Yea," I told him.

"My mom says you don't believe in Jesus Christ."

"No."

"You're going to hell."

There, it was that simple. I just shrugged my shoulders; what did I know? I was an eight-year-old kid.

The next one came in third grade. On the playground. With about five girls throwing a kickball back-and-forth to each other. Yes. Throwing. A *kick*ball.

By then, I'd started wearing these ridiculous glasses that made me look like a cross between Clark Kent and Shirley Temple. Not to mention, most adults tended to mistake me for some genius kid because I looked like a preschooler taking third-grade classes. I hated looking young.

"What religion are you?" the girl with the ball asked. She went down the line to each of us with her interrogation.

"Christian," the first girl said.

"Christian."

"Christian."

"Jewish."

The girl with the kickball stopped and looked me straight in the eyes. "You can't play with us," she told me, her voice nonchalant. "You're going to hell."

***

My first date was with my high school's German foreign exchange student. His name was Hans, and everyone used to call him a Nazi. It really pissed him off.

We were both sixteen and Hans was pretty cool; he was dark—not blond—because his mother was Italian. We used to talk about World War II on the phone and I'd tell him how my Polish family escaped just before Hitler took over. Hans couldn't get enough of my history, was fascinated by it. But he never told me much about his family.

We were never an item, never even kissed. But everyone used to joke how the Jew and the Nazi were going out. Hans was the first guy who treated me the same way he treated all the other cool kids who used to hang off his lanky arms like he was Leonardo DiCaprio. He smiled; he said my name when we passed each other in the halls; he laughed at my jokes (even when I wasn't trying).

But most of all, he was different. Like me.

A few years before I met Hans, I started coming to this gut realization that I'd never be able to date a typical American guy. He'd need to be from some distant, exotic land. Where maybe, just maybe, blond hair and blue eyes weren't such hot commodities.

I once asked Hans if he thought I was going to hell because I didn't believe in Jesus Christ. He just laughed over the phone, then said in a German accent, "Well, I am too. I don't believe in God."

***

I met Bahira in college, when I was writing for the school newspaper and sometimes spent my weekends with the local daily, shadowing its reporters. Bahira terrified me at first, with that Eastern European accent which struck fear deep into your bones. I suppose when you're an award-winning crime reporter, making the powerful cringe is a necessity.

"What kind of name is Alexis Schwartz?" she asked me when we first met.

"Jewish," I told her.

She didn't respond and just looked at me with those penetrating eyes, then walked away.

The newspaper editors told me to follow Bahira, and to my surprise, she enjoyed sharing her secrets with me. Like the best ways to search public records and find the money trail, then gather your information and interview the politician or CEO or police chief about your findings.

"The key," Bahira told me, "is to never let them know how much *you* know."

One day, I collected the nerve to ask Bahira how she learned so much, why the world didn't rattle her. *Nothing* rattled her, not even her editor-in-chief with his booming voice and deadline-throwing threats. That's when I learned about the war.

"You survived the Bosnian War?" I asked her.

"You can call it that ... yes," she said.

She told me about the camps, about the horrific massacres that stole the lives of her sister and father and best friend. She talked about the stench of death which gripped the city, and dodging bullets in the streets to grab a loaf of bread for her family. And of course, she spoke of the hate, all the hate.

"Hatred was not a strong enough word," she said. "Because we were Muslims, we didn't deserve to live. Later, after I'd left, I heard about a group of Serbs who'd burned down a house with people inside."

I merely sat next to Bahira in my rundown Honda Accord after she told me her story, staring out the scratched window while her fingers gripped the steering wheel until her knuckles turned white.

"They wanted you to go to hell because you were different," I finally said, still staring outside.

"No, Alexis," Bahira told me. "They didn't want us to go to hell. They created hell for us."

***

I stopped dying my hair blond when I turned twenty-five. I realized I'd been wandering this earth for a quarter of a century, and most people didn't know I was Jewish.

Suddenly, that bothered me.

I never left Arizona, as I'd planned since the day I was born. Once working in the newsroom, I met other outcasts of society: scientists, atheists, gay people, neurodivergents—all shunned by their peers and kicked off the kickball teams while growing up in the deserts of Phoenix.

They were condemned, like me.

In this place, I discovered my place among the discarded souls of our Wild West. A place where my eyeglasses and longer nose and dark spirals were welcomed with coffee and a half-assed smirk.

One day, while working a story, I ran into that kid, Carl, on the street—literally smashed into his shoulder while racing past him on the sidewalk with my coffee.

"Watch it!" he said, and I didn't recognize him until I followed the spilled coffee stains up to his collar, and finally met his eyes. They were still blue.

"Carl?" I asked.

The anger left his face momentarily, and confusion replaced it. "Do I know you?"

I glanced at my watch—I was running late—so I told him no, he didn't know me. The aggression returned, creeping up his cheeks into flushed circles.

"Go to hell," he said, then took off down the street and turned the corner.

I stood there and watched him scurry away. When I was sure he was out of earshot, I opened my mouth and spoke into the air.

"Gladly," I said. "Please, sign me up."

###

NON-FICTION ESSAYS AND PERSONAL NARRATIVES

• THOSE WERE THE DAYS •

> *"The ache for home lives in all of us. The safe place where we can go as we are and not be questioned."*
> **– Maya Angelou**

~~~

Outside my back window, a young family lives. They are Mexican.

The mother doesn't speak English. The two young girls speak English well, hardly exuding any sign of a Spanish accent. But then they turn to their mother and speak fluently in a language I cannot understand.

They are perhaps nine and seven, and they already speak more languages than me—a twenty-four-year-old college graduate who's working as a professional journalist.

The little girls are sweet and well-behaved. The other day, one of them had a birthday. As I rested on my backyard couch, under the awning of my duplex, they walked up and offered me wildflowers.

"Here, this is for my birthday," the youngest one said.
~~~

I smiled and thanked her, finding the youngest especially adorable. She's a fragile thing, with thick, wavy black hair falling the length of her back. She encompasses all that is innocent in this life.

However, it's none of this which makes me sad.

It's watching the family together, as a whole—happy. The father grounds his hands and knees into the backyard dirt, digging a hole to plant fresh bushes. The youngest girl sips a homemade drink while the oldest rests atop their porch and grins, watching her father. The mother stands over her husband, and I see them smile at each other. This reminds me of my carefree days as a child, when nothing mattered and everything was perfect.

Those were the days when I would come home from school, grab my little sister and run outside onto our front lawn. Those were the days when throwing sticks into a tree, hoping they would latch between the branches, was all it took to feel content.

I imagine those two little girls feel carefree as they run and play dress-up in their backyard after school. I'm sure the youngest is the "girly-girl," always dressed in cutesy outfits with her hair tied in ribbons. On the other hand, the older sister is down to earth. She doesn't care for make-up and worries more about her friends than boys.

But most of all, I imagine their security. When they come home from school, Mom is greeting them with afternoon sandwiches. Dad shows his face an hour later, happy to see his girls after work.

They remind me of my sister and me in our younger years—during Hanukkah when we'd relentlessly tear apart the wrapping paper hiding our gifts, then smile after finding secret treasures inside. We'd watch cartoons by the fireplace, sing along with our favorite songs and eat gelt. During the summertime, we'd hop around our backyard pool with Dad, bouncing around a blow-up beach ball, trying to keep it from touching the water. Mom would come outside and sit in a chair with a camera and take pictures.

Yes, those were the days.

But not anymore. I wonder if what I see in the family living behind me is a façade. Will someday, those girls grow up and learn the truth? Will someday, they search everywhere for a place that feels like home, but never find it?

Or perhaps, does home truly exist?

Perhaps the closest we can feel to home is in our memories, back before any of us really *knew*. Perhaps we all live in a dream, in a fantasy world, until one day we just grow up.

The family behind me cooks barbeques. I have a barbeque in my backyard. Barbeques are never fun alone. So, I never fire the grill. It just sits out there, wondering when someone will turn its knob and light the flame.

My dad used to cook barbeques in the old days, especially during summer. We invited family friends over. My sister, my friends and I swam all afternoon until the skin on our fingers and toes turned to prunes. As the afternoon came to close, the scent of barbeque smoke filled the air surrounding us. It was electric.

Today, I don't celebrate Hanukkah consistently anymore. My dad doesn't believe in gifts and my mom is too busy to make major plans. This year for Thanksgiving, I'll probably spend it with my mom. My father and sister will travel to California to visit my grandma, and I'd hate to leave Mom alone. I've never had a Thanksgiving with just one other person before.

It's amazing how small a family can become.

When I watch the little neighbor girls play outside in their backyard, I realize my past feels like a dream that never happened. I think back to those early days of full families and secure nights, and I wonder, *Was that ever me?*

###

• CRACKS IN THE WALL •

"I see the world being slowly transformed into a wilderness, I hear the approaching thunder that, one day, will destroy us too, I feel the suffering of millions."

– Anne Frank

~~~

In America, you live in a movie. But then you come to Israel, to the Middle East, and you see reality.

Amir's words still echo in my mind today, after eight years from that evening in a cramped hotel room, crossed knees jammed against crossed knees, an acoustic guitar resting next to Amir's lap.

It was January 2009 when I first travelled to Israel, at the height of Operation Cast Lead—known as the Gaza Crisis ... a crisis so bloody, no one within the walls of Jerusalem or Tel Aviv would speak of it. The lesson I'd learned on that trip now echoes in my thoughts, among the rhetoric that has come to plague my beloved America in 2017.

However, eight years ago in that hotel room, my mind drifted back only days earlier, when I stood upon the vortex
~~~

of merging worlds—watching the sun set from the stone ground of an Israeli military base, gazing over barbed wire into the West Bank.

Staring at the Wall.

A mosque, draped in white purity and exuding a green ambiance from the crowning dome, topped a nearby hill. As the sunset's warmth enveloped the Arab town, protected by its towering mosque, men's evening prayers echoed throughout the hilltops in a mesmerizing harmony.

Just below, the great Wall extended into the horizon, separating the Jewish sector from the Arab prayers above.

Images of bloodied faces and flaming buses on the news flashed through my mind from childhood, then: *Another suicide bomber killed 50 people on a public bus in Jerusalem today.* And subsequently, I thought of the stories our Jewish tour guide told, of playing Russian roulette with his children, of debating every day whether to take the bus or his car. *Which had a better chance of survival?* he would ask.

I sometimes forget: the word "God" makes humans do crazy things.

On this evening upon an Israeli military base, I stood above the Wall, allowing the gentle choir of Arab voices to hypnotize me. Such peace, such beauty.

We don't like this town, a female voice spoke from behind me then, jerking me from my trance. It was our travel mate who lived on this military base. *Many terrorists live there, and we've had many problems with them.*

The reality sunk into my head, and before another image or thought could sweep my mind, I thought of Mirsada.

Mirsada, a Muslim woman who never lived in the Middle East, but grew up in Bosnia. Who intimidated not only me when I first met her as a rookie twenty-three-year-old newspaper reporter, but terrified every cop within a twenty-mile radius with that dominant eastern European accent.

I remember clearly, they used to call her "Bulldog."

Perhaps that's why Mirsada earned several *Associated Press* awards as our paper's lead crime reporter. It was because of Mirsada that I have my investigation and interrogation skills today. But I learned much more from her than important reporting techniques.

I learned that pacifism has power.

Mirsada lost her brother to genocide during the Bosnian War, and she spent thirteen days as a prisoner in a Serb concentration camp. She thought she'd escaped the propaganda associated with the word "Muslim" by coming to America, until a tumultuous 2016 presidential election reverberated those fears in her mind.

Mirsada, however, is not one to buckle under fear. She dove into the streets and dodged sniper fire to train as a runner for the 1992 Barcelona Olympics for Bosnia's first Olympic team. Amidst the chaos of a war-torn Sarajevo, Mirsada raced through the roads as Serb militants sprayed bullets into the city from hilltops above. Slicing through the silence, only gunshots piercing the air, Mirsada dashed by blocked alleys and shelled buildings, skintight eighties running leggings wrapped around her legs.

You could not hear or see a bird in the air, Mirsada would later tell me. *It was almost like death had enveloped the city, and even wildlife understood the danger. It felt as if the world had stopped moving.*

But Mirsada refused to stop. She ran because she wanted the world to see what was happening to her country. The hope of intervention, of action from the major powers, drove her like a lightning bolt through the streets of Sarajevo. Soon, the *Associated Press* picked up Mirsada's story and her face spread across the globe, making it to the cover of *Reader's Digest*.

Now, decades later, after stories of childhood friends turning guns on her and her family, after memories of Serbs tearing apart her life, Mirsada hasn't let these people define her future. She gathered her despair and began a new life in America—having children, finishing her degree, mentoring rookie reporters. Yet today, I watch as her fears return, and I realize something.

As I stood upon the Israeli military base and stared at the Wall eight years ago, I recalled whispers of Israeli Arabs treated as second class citizens. The stories of my Jewish guide's Russian roulette with his children then intermingled with those whispers. I thought of my ex-boyfriend, who grew to detest me after several years because I'm Jewish. I almost never took my birthright trip to Israel, because of him.

Mirsada lost her brother, her home, her people, because of that Wall. I almost lost my identity because of that Wall. And I realized, this snaking, overbearing Wall extends far beyond Jerusalem.

People in Israel talk of breaking down the Wall, but I stood on the vortex of two worlds that evening, staring into the sunset while only miles away, a war raged in Gaza. Amir was right. In America, we have lived in a movie. Perhaps, in 2017, we're finally beginning to face the reality. We must not allow that Wall to invade us, too.

My Muslim friend, Mirsada, began chipping at the Wall's structure by running through the streets of her under-siege city, rather than returning the firepower. She began by fighting to live her life, her way. And she began by teaching a young, Jewish reporter about the power of rising above.

Should that power gain enough force, the next time I travel to Israel, I might find a crack in the Wall. And I'll smile.

###

• DEATH OF A DREAM •

> *"You must create the right kind of dream, the sober, adult kind of magic: illusion born from disillusion."*
>
> **– Sylvia Plath**

~~~

They say to lose your dreams is to lose hope, and hope is what inspires us to live.

I guess you can say that's what happened to me. Except my dreams didn't just die. They were murdered.

I never entered journalism with the expectation my degree would become obsolete only five years after graduating in 2005. If newspapers had thrived for the past two hundred years, what made anyone think they'd falter then?

The first two years out of college, I lived the dream. Maybe I wasn't writing for the *New York Times* or the *Washington Post*, but I was the lead education reporter on a small-town daily. During those years, I earned two *Associated Press* awards as part of an investigative news team.
~~~

Journalism made my blood rage like the white waters down the Colorado. I thrived off the hunt for the truth; I reveled in confronting politicians or board members when they had something to hide. Locals would tell me I had a talent for reporting. An old colleague of Peter Jennings offered to write me a recommendation letter for Columbia University's journalism master's degree.

And then, everything changed.

***

If I could have traveled back in time to when I left the newspaper in late 2007, I would have caused my younger self a stroke. At the time, I was preparing to move back home to Phoenix, Arizona. That's where my boyfriend and family lived, and I missed them.

I figured I'd snatch a job on one of the newspapers in the Valley. Easy, right? I started applying, and applying, and applying. But as the foreclosures began sealing around me like a snake squeezing air from my lungs, the papers told me the same thing:

"Sorry, we're on a hiring freeze."

They later said it was some sort of "housing bubble burst," and I realized if I wanted to move back to Phoenix,

I'd have to leave journalism. Not permanently, but for a bit. In the meantime, I'd find a job on "the dark side."

Public relations.

Even muttering the words made me shudder. Journalists *hated* PR people. They represented everything journalism fought to expose. And here I was, contemplating becoming one of them.

I didn't know it at the time, but I'd wind up working in PR longer than I ever worked as a reporter. And with the Great Recession just around the corner, I'd never be a journalist again.

***

It was January 2008 when I made the switch. Only six months later, I heard my old newspaper started layoffs.

In my reporting job, I spent seventy percent of my day outside, driving my car, and talking with sources from school board presidents to the state treasurer. Once I started in PR, I had to ask permission before calling people within the company. I spent all day inside a cubicle.

Within the year, I started searching for journalism jobs. The economy was bound to turn around soon, and something would open. Right?

Another year passed, then another.

Suddenly, I found myself trapped in a career I never wanted, in a profession my subconscious rejected. Yet my skills and education as a journalist would only allow me to work in PR. Unless I returned to school for a new degree, I had no other option.

I wasn't naïve. I realized my PR job allowed me to buy a house while others lost their homes. The work kept me employed while my neighbors returned without a job. The company, and the profession, became my dry mountaintop amidst a deadly flood.

I didn't know whether to be thankful or angry. So finally, I decided. I became depressed.

***

I hit the wall a few years later when I realized I was never going back. I saw myself sitting in a cubicle until the age of sixty-five, slaving away in Corporate America, and I gave up—on everything.

Then one night, during a conversation with my boyfriend, things changed.

"Use them to better you," he told me, referring to my employer and the PR skills I had to develop. "Use it to better yourself, as a writer."

Writer? I hadn't thought of myself as a writer, just a journalist. But then I remembered I first fell in love with writing at the age of seven, when I composed my first story about a girl who befriended aliens named after foods. I wasn't a reporter then, just a creative writer.

Yes! I thought. *I can work on becoming an author. Why not?* At my job, we were forced into learning everything social media and marketing. Maybe, just maybe, if I tried embracing those concepts, I could use them to promote myself as a writer and break free.

Suddenly, I couldn't learn enough. I started my own blog. I set up a Twitter account. I dove head-first into the tech world and read everything I could on how to network via cyberspace.

In just a few months, I gained 22,000 hits to my blog. I wound up with 230 email subscribers, nearly 370 Twitter followers, and launched a Facebook page for myself as an author.

***

I soon found myself connecting with other writers who were working toward the Dream but couldn't navigate the tech revolution our world was facing. They didn't understand it, and they found themselves left behind.

It was my blog, my writing, my tips, that helped them start their own path. I couldn't believe what I'd done. I, Shari Lopatin, managed to inspire *others*.

Being my own writer has become my new dream. I'm not quite there yet, but I'm the closest I've ever come. And though it was hard, I buried my dreams of becoming a well-known journalist.

Sometimes, the longing wells up and I wish I could become a reporter again. The feeling reminds me of saying good-bye to a loved one who died. Once I learn to let go, I can move on, but sometimes the memories resurface, and I hurt again.

But to lose your dreams is to lose hope, and hope is what inspires us to live. I'm not sure what tomorrow holds, but I plan on living a long, long time.

###

• THE DAY GOD STOLE MY COMPUTER •

> *"Life is what happens while you are busy making other plans."*
>
> **– John Lennon**

~~~

I didn't realize how much sleep I'd been losing or notice the extra few pounds puffing around my face.

Until one Monday in April.

That's the day God stole my computer, forcing me to take a break from the world of technology that was consuming my life. It's the day God said, "Slow down! You're forgetting how to *live.*"

It's the day God disguised himself as a group of unruly teenagers looking for trouble; who tested their stupidity and left fingerprints on my broken kitchen window for the police; who ransacked my house, terrified my cats, stole my incense lighters (yes, *all* my lighters).

And finally—took my computer.

Really, being a writer, I don't own much else of value. I don't even have cable. This is why my after-work hours
~~~

became devoted to another type of labor: self-promotion. After all, isn't that what every writer is doing nowadays?

Updating blogs. Prepping tweets and Facebook posts. Writing guest posts. Building that author platform for the book they'll finish—as soon as they lure enough followers—because unless they're Judy Blume or Nora Roberts or Stephen King, they're like me:

A few articles published locally and nationally, using my former days as a newspaper reporter to entice editors, working a nine-to-five job getting paid to write for some company, freelancing for magazines in my spare hours. But what I *really* dream about, what *really* pumps my blood, is making it big on the *New York Times* Bestseller's List.

However, amid working toward all this, I forgot one small tidbit—to live.

After God stole my computer, I found myself forced to read a classic novel while relaxing on the sofa. I spent more time with my cats tossing fuzzy toy mice around my kitchen floor. I even went to sleep before eleven o'clock and awoke at five in the morning for some treadmill time. Best of all, I re-wrote my stolen narrative for the 2011 *Writer's Digest* Competition the old-fashioned way:

Using pen and paper.

That's when it hit me. Building that name, that voice, that presence is so important for the success writers crave, that I forgot the most essential aspect of writing is living.

As angry as I was when I discovered my ransacked home, I suppose I should thank those careless teenagers who stole my incense lighters. After buying a new computer, I contemplated leaving it with a trusted friend once every few months to remove temptation and force me back into life.

In fact, after reintroducing a laptop to my home, part of me felt sad. I actually *enjoyed* not having the option to hop onto the World Wide Web.

I suppose God knew what was best for me, after all, that Monday in April.

###

• A NEUROTIC'S TAKE ON DATING •

> *"It will never be perfect, but perfect is overrated."*
> **– Tina Fey**

~~~

What is it about dating that gives me a conniption? Is it the pressure to plump that amazing, magical good-night kiss? Is it the guy's expectation that I really am the person he met the first time?

'Cause, I'm not.

I'm neurotic, klutzy, talkative. I stumble over my words when I become nervous. I even giggle, God help me.

Maybe it's the fact I've never really dated before. I'm twenty-four and been out with one person. Yes, we were together for a number of years, but I think guys have radar for this kind of inexperience. And I have radar for their radar. Most likely, this is why I trip over myself when a guy makes my heart skip a beat, although, that doesn't happen too often.

I have this dream occasionally that I'm out somewhere in public, and I'm talking to someone I want to impress. Out
~~~

of nowhere, my front tooth falls out. I have two fake teeth in real life, so this dream is actually nightmarish. There I am, covering my mouth and slipping my tongue over toothless gums, hoping I'm just dreaming (talk about an answered prayer). All the while, I'm continuing to laugh and flirt as if nothing happened, like the guy can't notice my wicked, witchy grin.

I love being single. Seriously. I have a lot of fun flirting around and remaining unattached. But if it comes to getting involved, I want to skip the first four months and hop right into "I can act like an idiot and you'll think it's cute." Dating, on the other hand . . . no.

The whole thing is like one big job interview. If you show up late, the other person is already wondering whether you're reliable. If you're not wearing the right clothes for the occasion, your date starts wondering if you're socially adaptable. You better know the right answers to all the right questions, and you need to be smooth.

Smooth?

I don't know the meaning of the word. My friends and family say my life is filled with "Shari moments." I even met my ex-boyfriend by spilling spaghetti onto the carpet, slipping, and then falling into my own mess.

That relationship ended badly. I can only imagine what will happen next. My future husband will probably hit me with his car.

Perhaps the reason I have trouble finding dates is because when I meet a guy I like, I tend to act more like a friend. It's safer that way. If men think they're ridiculously scared of rejection, they haven't met me.

###

• THE COURAGE TO FORGIVE MYSELF •

> *"The weak can never forgive. Forgiveness is the attribute of the strong."*
>
> **– Mahatma Gandhi**

~~~

I can remember the first time he said my Jewish heritage bothered him: it was the night before September 11—Sept. 10, 2001.

I awoke to smoking towers in more ways than one the following day. We'd been together for a year, and he'd celebrated one Hanukkah with my family. Yet, when I refused to convert to his religion, Christianity, he called Jews arrogant.

I should have broken it off that night. However, I was nineteen years old and he was my first relationship. When he apologized a few days later, I told myself it was a slip of the tongue and we moved on.

I'd always been proud of my Jewish heritage; my mother had family who died in the Holocaust, and my Jewish grandfather fought the Nazis in World War II. As a kid, I
~~~

reveled in watching the envy drip from my classmates' eyes as I bragged about my eight nights of gifts every December. At age fourteen, I became a Bat Mitzvah and shared the celebration with dozens of friends from school and dance, bouncing through life, wearing my Star of David necklace with pride—and then I met him.

I was the first Jew he'd known. Perhaps it was because I was different than other girls, but he found my ways both fascinating and intriguing.

It felt surreal when he later called Jews arrogant, but his apology calmed my fears. Like all toxic trends, however, it didn't end there. It never does.

He soon asked if I'd attend church, and I said sure, if he would try temple. He refused. Then, he asked if I'd consider becoming a Jew for Jesus, but later recanted, saying I'd have to surrender everything Jewish, even eating challah. He loved me, he said, "But I can't marry you because you're not Christian."

I wanted him to marry me. His approval somehow dwarfed into this looming, unattainable ideal that I'd been pursuing my entire life. I sought it while trying not to betray myself, and his anger grew.

"You're being selfish," he would tell me when I wanted to spend Rosh Hashanah—the Jewish New Year—with my mother. "You're choosing your family and your heritage over me. I thought you loved me."

Then, the research started. He became obsessed with the idea that I wasn't Jewish, that my bloodline was strictly Russian and Polish and had been converted to Judaism. He spent hours on the computer, printing information from so-called historical sites that proved his point. He told me the New Testament was supposed to replace the Old Testament, and Judaism is a religion that should no longer exist.

I couldn't challenge his delusions without regressing into a fight, so I let him lay the "facts and figures" before me, month after month. I felt ashamed—maybe I was being selfish, maybe he had a point—and slowly, I started to doubt my own heritage, my own family bloodline.

It ended one weekend after more than five years, when he admitted he no longer loved me, and I told him I wanted to die. The next day, I called a pastor to convert to Christianity, then drove to his house, but he looked at me with cold eyes and said, "It's too late. Why didn't you do this before?"

I stopped eating and shrunk to one hundred pounds, wanting nothing to do with Jewish culture for fear new friends would detest me. Over the coming months, I hiked my way out of despair through the mountains of Prescott, and a year later, I met Oscar.

"You're Jewish?" he asked when I revealed my background. "Tell me about it!" But I refused, the overwhelming shame washing over me.

One day, while visiting my mom's house, Oscar wanted to watch my Bat Mitzvah tape. In front of my mother, I said no. Oscar couldn't understand my hesitation, and later that day, I broke into convulsive tears, unable to pinpoint the emotion that surged.

"You're angry at yourself for turning your back on your culture," Oscar said. "You have to forgive yourself."

You have to forgive yourself. Never had truer words been spoken.

At first, forgiving myself implied I had done something wrong, and I couldn't face the possibility that I played a part in allowing this overpowering denial to happen. Yet deep in my subconscious, I knew Oscar was right: my only path to peace was self-forgiveness.

I spoke to myself in the quiet of dark and replayed memories like a broken movie. I acknowledged what he had done, then accepted my role—maybe I was weak, or naïve, or blind—but none of it changed the ultimate truth.

I tumbled through this abyss until, like the sunrise welcoming day, I found the courage to say it. "I forgive you, Shari."

In a year, I would find myself standing at the West Wall in Jerusalem—the last remnants of the original Temple of Solomon—with a dampened and crumpled prayer in the palm of my hand, crying alongside my Jewish travel mates against aged bricks.

This was my birthright, and I had seized it with the fervor of the Maccabees or the Jews following Moses. The Wall towered over my small body, and as I laid my hand upon its rough surface, I felt the presence of my parents, and their parents, and their parents, and their parents, and their parents, and their parents, and their parents, and theirs ...

###

POETRY

Lindsay – The Brightest Star

There was once a young girl,
Eyes black as night,
Soul gray as dusk,
But a heart full of light.
Her wit enchanted
Any spark to fire,
With beauty that bewitched
Any grief into glamour.

Such devils which threatened
To capture her soul,
She gallantly fought
'Till her victory unfold.
A quiet bud
Which bloomed to a flower,
Many she loved,
But more love surrounded her.

The brightest star,
Which burns out too quick,
Is still the brightest,
And the one we pick.
That brightest star,

Even though gone,
Burns strong in our minds,
And that light lives on.

Let gaps be filled
With zestful light,
Despair pushed on
With her will to fight.
Our souls be lightened
With her enchanted wit,
And grief brought to glamour,
For her beauty we lit.

The brightest stars,
They steal the sky,
Filled with wonder, passion,
And truth over lies.
When they're gone,
Even though not seen,
Never burn out,
Forever they gleam.

The War Within (Confusion)

***A note from the author before reading this poem**

I wrote "The War Within (Confusion)" when I was fifteen years old, as part of an assignment for English class. After I turned it in, my English teacher announced to the class she received one assignment that encompassed the essence of what she was looking for in a poem.

She promised to keep the author anonymous, then proceeded to read my work aloud. I was flabbergasted, but also immensely embarrassed. I heard gasps from my classmates as she continued reading my words.

After she finished, my teacher said, "Would the author like to reveal him or herself?" I remained quiet, terrified that once my classmates learned these private thoughts were mine, they'd laugh. My teacher gave me one more chance, but I remained silent.

Today, at forty-one years old, I am publishing that poem and proclaiming to the world that I, Shari Lopatin, am the proud author.

I sit in my room,
Shut in behind closed doors,
And my life spins right before me,
As I lay on my bed with closed eyes.

My life is a war,
And I am the enemy.
Fighting myself in this never-ending battle,
I will not win, nor lose.

I feel like there's two of me,
And I'm not sure which one to be.
I'm playing a tug-of-war game
And neither side is budging.

And so I sit and think:
When will this war end?
When will this game stop?
And I become wrapped up
In deeper
Confusion.

Unseen

Whose is that voice which calls me?
Lures me into a dream?
It lifts me and surrounds me,
Emboldens and defines me,
And yet his face is unseen.

Whose are those eyes which watch me?
Delving into my soul?
They capture and defy me,
Haunt me to oblivion,
And yet they remain unknown.

Whose are those hands which touch me?
Burning my heart to fire?
Their light, feathery whispers
Driving me mad with desire.

Whose is that breath which warms me?
Caressing as he breathes?
It seduces and empowers me,
It melts and yet it strengthens me,
But still his face is unseen.

Rainy Day

Come hither,
Oy joyous tears,
Which seek to drench my soul
In such glistening raindrops,
Which God sprinkles upon my brow.
For even though Heaven's tears
Soak my flesh, I smile above,
Radiant with such sadness
Which leaks from nature's divine eyes.
I welcome the scolding
Of God's angry tyrants,
Their voices echoing, ferocious in their wake,
Over the mountains and past the horizon.
But never as much shall I grin,
As I do now,
Into the ocean of grayness,
Which sings to my soul's beautiful hymn.

Sweet Delirium

The world is my ride,
A trip to the Heavens.
Floating, flying,
Twirling to my garden,
Where every secret
Is trapped,
And held,
And mysteriously opening
To sweet delirium.

It is nothing,
And everything,
Understood,
And confused.
But uncaring I dance,
And I swing, and I dive,
Over and over
To my sweet delirium.

Reality is a dream,
Truth becomes past.
Every world, and land,

Merge to my dream
Of nothing,
And everything,
Floating and flying,
Then drowning in swirls
Of my sweet delirium.

The Other Side

Dwelling in the psyche of my mind,
Swimming in the heart of my soul,
Confusion overtakes to make me blind.
I cannot find
The cure to my soul,
Never so bold,
To find its way to the other side.

Drowning in the depth of despair,
Choking from the grip of fate,
Me being, overtaken by its fear,
It would not hear
My cry of hate;
For Heaven's sake!
Dear God, where is the other side?

Lost in a maze of pure anxiety,
Falling through the hole of naked deceit,
I desperately search for true prosperity;
Instead find impurity.
And so I flee,
For I cannot see
The Truth in myself,
Leading toward the other side.

Fire and Ice

It began,
The smallest of burns,
The dimmest of pricks,
But gradually it grew
Above the rest.
Piercing, burning,
Tearing me apart—
It yearns and it blows
To destroy and entice,
Raging over me,
The fire and ice.

It flows
As the river,
Sweeping all in its path.
It dives
As the waves,
Drowning the helpless.
Striving, screaming,
Shredding my soul—
It yearns and it blows
To destroy and entice,
Raging over me,
The fire and ice.

Saved?

If there's a Heaven,
Will I go?

If I don't believe,
But love thy neighbor,
Shall I ascend
To Heaven?

If I disobey,
Break the rules,
Ride the highs,
Ignore the lows,
But part the skin
To find the soul,
Will I go to Heaven?

If I don't pretend
To live a lie,
If I search for faith,
At least I tried.
But I want to know,
Is it true?

Will I be forgiven?
Will I be loved?
If after the facades and greed,
Will I at least rise above?
Do I get a chance,
Even if I'm not sure?

'Cause after all,
If God discriminates,
What else is there to live for?

My Ecstasy

I feel it melt,
Then caress my tongue.
I tingle so sweet,
My taste but one.
I crave its warmth,
Fill my veins,
Its velvet touch
Brings such shame!
It moves across
To tantalize,
My tastebuds twitch,
I agonize!
But oh its richness,
Though forbidden,
This chocolate thrills me!
Keep it hidden ...

Shadow Dancer

She twirls, she prances,
She sways in the wind.
Such heavenly dances,
With naught but a grin.
Her heart, it cries,
From shadows in the night,
A love song of lies,
A once stolen life.
His eyes, they are blind—
His lips, they are sealed—
She searches to find
Her love, she must yield.
But why, she then asks,
Am I empty to him?
I need hide by my mask,
I so quietly sin.
And yet she goes on,
Through darkness of meadows,
With her love never gone,
She dances in shadows.

Sacred Day

It's Christmas Day and here I sit,
Whilst long-drawn shadows and silent quilts.
I wonder what the families sing,
Of toys, of bread, or their newborn King?
My cat, he whines at the windowsill.
He begs for freedom in an unknown field.
Such solitude in beauty's wake,
Be blessing or curse, I dare not make.
My mind falls cradled to palms of warmth,
My sight drifts shut, my soul sails forth.
I journey toward another world,
Where clothes and cars forsake our hold.

What beauty doth the mean green make?
Such Things bring happiness we're forced to fake.
Freedom's song lies beyond the coin,
Where truth, and soul, and conscience join.
An unheard voice cries to the air,
"What happened to the land I bear?
No more shall the sun rise in the East,
It's fallen prey to my mutant beast."

Suddenly, my peaceful being
Is clawing down a spiral, screaming.
What happened to my Earth, my beam,
To Man's last hope of salvation's dream?
For the solitude I dare not cry,
Amidst such greed for gold am I.
By means of such a sacred day,
We've doomed ourselves to Man's decay.

Behind the Wall

Just beyond the wall of greed,
Your touch awaits my hold,
My need.
I stare above, translucent guides,
I wonder where you sit,
You hide.
Does your mind wander
Toward thoughts of clouds?
Or yearn for waves of fire,
Of shrouds?
I beg to know,
Where are you now?
My lips, they call your name—
I'm found.
I wait with wanton,
I yearn to see,
Come down and save the last of me.

Kiss

I love the way
My name
Falls from your lips,
And the warmth
You breathe
As we kiss.

For Aleppo

The earth, it trembles
As they fall like rain,
But I can do no more
Than weep
And cast my disdain.
May the rainbows dance
In the glitter beyond,
And the sunlight sing
To welcome Aleppo
At last, in eternity.

America, How I Weep

Oh America,
How I weep for thee!
My once beautiful muse,
My distant refuge.
Your maternal embrace
Protected our grace, and welcomed
My family whole.

But now I stand atop your dream,
In cowardice and fear I glean ...
We watch with haste,
Such distaste,
And mourn the death of hope
And faith.

America, when will you rise?
And crush the hate which I despise?
With this prayer,
I say to thee,
Revive the truth in us, in me.

The Color Red

What happens when
You reach the color red?
And veins of poison
Fill your blood with dread?

Will demons churn your gut
Into curry-drizzled bait,
Imploring other devils
To feast on mounds of hate?

No matter how you turn
From the final specs of dusk,
They'll seek you in your sleep,
They'll trick you as you lust.

The thunder looms nearby now,
Consuming in your head,
And there is no more running
From the woeful color red.

Pieces of You – For Grandma

As days pass by
And time moves on
I watch as
Pieces of you
Fall away
One by one.

First your smile
Then your laugh.
Your words of comfort
And your dreams
Of the past.

Your chair today,
Your tree tomorrow.
Then I watch
As my childhood
Fades into sorrow.

Linda

It was winter,
Or maybe it was spring.
How could I remember,
When such thoughts are blurred
By eyes that wept,
Over a coffin that held
My second mother,
As she slept.

I was five,
But could've been ten.
It didn't really matter
When all I knew,
Is I loved, then lost.
She was here, then gone.
Mommy? I would ask,
When's she coming back?
But silence I received
From a grief beyond
What I could see.

It was summer,
Or maybe it was fall.

But either way I looked,

I just couldn't get it.

Linda wasn't coming back,

Not anymore

Not at all.

The Chaos of Question

The chaos of question,
The anxiety of why,
They eat at my pain –
I suffer,
I cry.

The angst of confusion,
The moment of truth.
It's hidden away –
I search,
I sleuth.

The answers await
Beyond the closed door.
They tease at my senses –
I hunger,
I scorn.

But I clasp to the hope,
Inspired by faith,
Patience breeds mercy –
So I beg,
And I wait.

But still my relief
Lingers beyond sight.
The chaos of question –
It consumes
My might.

Always There

In the darkest hours
And deepest days,
From the hardest hardship
That may break my way,
He stands above
To hold my hand,
And remind me that
I can.

He never leaves,
He always loves,
The best Dad
A daughter could ever
Think of.

I love you Dad,
And just like you,
I'll always be there
To see you
Through and through.

A Marine at My Door

It was Monday afternoon.
A Marine approached my door.
He handed me a folded flag,
He bowed his head in soft dolor.
But I don't know who died, I said,
I don't know a Marine.
4102 was the address, he showed,
But not the same street.

It was Monday afternoon
When I helped a Marine outside.
A solemn message he held still
For an unknown face,
An unknown cry.
I searched and sought and found
For him,
The other house engraved
With the numbers on my front porch
So he could drive away.

He took his folded flag with him
In a dignified part.
And that Monday afternoon,
I knew,
A Marine would break a heart.

Why I Write

Because the moon shines bright
But tonight
I don't care.
It died for me
One summer dawn.

Because the world screams
In similes
And dreams.
But none of us
Can hear, nor try.

Because sometimes I ache
With a despondent
Grace
That I hide inside
My daily work face.

Because we all need
Something to believe
As our tongues betray
What we yearn
To say.

And because nothing
Makes sense, and we live
In pretense.
So I write, I write, I write –
And I fight.

• ABOUT THE AUTHOR •

Read more of Shari Lopatin's work and be the first to learn about new books by signing up for Shari's newsletter as either a free or paid subscriber: *sharilopatin.substack.com.*

~~~

Shari Lopatin writes stories that matter. An award-winning journalist in her earlier years, she now writes novels that tie into modern-day social issues, serialized fiction, short stories, personal and political essays, and poetry.

Over the course of her seventeen-plus year career, Shari has worked as a newspaper reporter, magazine writer, public relations professional, social media manager, and earned the title of "Cat Mom of the Year." She published her debut novel, *The Apollo Illusion*, in 2018 and lives in Phoenix, Arizona, where she was born and raised.
~~~

www.ingramcontent.com/pod-product-compliance
Lightning Source LLC
Chambersburg PA
CBHW071005120726
47910CB00004B/1393

* 9 7 8 0 9 9 9 7 8 2 7 3 6 *